Get More Lead

In

Your Pencil

Maxine Gregg

ISBN: 978-1-7764175-2-0

DEDICATION

This book is dedicated to Lynette Mary

Disclaimer

The information presented is not intended to diagnose, treat, or cure any medical condition or disease. It is not intended to replace a relationship with your medical doctor. It is for educational and informational purposes only, based on information from reputable studies and experience from experts in the field. The book has not been evaluated by the FDA.

What makes you male. (As opposed to female...Duh)

A quick overview of hormones.

This is going to get a bit technical but it's worth reading because interspersed among the boring biological info, are little gems that will help to sustain a rock- hard penis and amazing stamina… so bear with me.

Hormones are our body's messengers. They are chemicals produced by various glands whose job it is to carry instructions in the body so our bodily functions can work smoothly. They are the foundation of communication in our body, without which there would be chaos. But like any communication system, accurate translation of the message is imperative and relies on healthy hormones, as well as whether our cells are capable of even hearing the message. So, ensuring these messengers carry the correct instruction is important for smooth functioning. (Sadly, there are many processes that interrupt the correct message).

The name given to the whole system that makes up our hormones is: The Endocrine System.

The Endocrine System

The main hormone producing glands (and the effect in our body) are:

Pituitary: Considered the "master control gland," this gland controls other glands and makes the hormones that trigger growth.

Hypothalamus: Another master gland responsible for body temperature, hunger, moods, and the release of hormones from other glands; Balanced sleep and libido are influenced by the hypothalamus

Parathyroid: Important for balancing the amount of calcium exchanged within the cells.

Thymus: Responsible for our immunity.

Pancreas: A hard working gland producing insulin (helps control blood sugar). It also produces digestive enzymes.

Thyroid: The thyroid produces hormones associated with metabolic rate (energy), heart rate, temperature control and a sense of wellbeing.

Adrenal: Adrenal glands produce sex hormones in both men and women and cortisol thus contributing to sex drive and stress management. Stress impacts heavily on our other glands and organs.

Pineal (my favourite) Also called the thalamus, this gland produces serotonin and its derivative, melatonin, which affects sleep.

Ovaries: Only in women, (duh) the ovaries secrete oestrogen, testosterone (yes really) and progesterone (more please), the female sex hormones.

Testes: Only in men, the testes produce the male sex hormone, testosterone, and produce sperm.

Activity: Nothing. You did what you needed to just reading the info.

Testosterone 101:

Men associate their 'maleness' with testosterone and this is, of course, true but it isn't the whole story. The ability to feel that tooth grinding pleasure, as well as have a fully functioning tool (pardon me) to prolong and enjoy it, depends on a mixed bag of hormones and enzymes.

How is testosterone made in your body?

Firstly, testosterone needs cholesterol, (so for those of you who are on a statin for high cholesterol, if you have lost your libido or are having erectile problem, chat to your doctor about this. You may not have enough cholesterol for your hormones). The pituitary gland (see above) triggers luteinizing hormone and LH stimulates the production of pregnenolone (remember this name. It comes up later) from the cholesterol, which then makes dehydroepiandrostone (DHEA)… Really, who the hell thinks of these words? And this makes testosterone, mostly from the testes.

However, while the effects we crave are from the free testosterone, there are two metabolites that are made from testosterone that affect how much free testosterone you have left to use. One is called DHT (dihydrotestosterone: Seriously??!!!) and the other is oestradiol. (The hormone associated with PMT; I kid you not)

Free testosterone is converted to DHT via an enzyme called 5-alpha reductase and to oestradiol by an enzyme called aromatase. In the case of too little free testosterone, it is possible to block both of these enzymes using various modalities but because the natural balance of hormones in the body is quite sensitive, it is not advisable to hammer the process unduly yourself. Get some advice on this.

1. SHBG. Sex hormone binding globulin. This is a hormone that binds testosterone and prevents it from being used. (Bad news for rock-hard erections) So, when SHBG is holding lots of testosterone, there is only a tiny bit left for the cells to use, as only FREE testosterone can be used. As one ages, SHBG increases, holding on to more testosterone. While is seems like a good idea to lower SHBG and free up testosterone, too little SHBG can result in acne and mood swings in men. SHBG also binds to oestrogen (and men also have oestrogen) so if you lower the SHBG, there will also be more free oestrogen in your system. Generally, SHBG in adult men is fairly stable but insulin resistance and obesity both lower SHBG, thus increasing the free oestrogen and further putting a man at risk for erectile dysfunction (jeez… a double whammy) because of the excess oestrogen. This is a vicious cycle.
2. 5-alpha-reductase. This is an enzyme that converts testosterone to DHT (associated with hair loss) and therefore also reduces the amount of free, usable testosterone.
3. Aromatase. This is an enzyme that converts testosterone to oestradiol (one of the forms of oestrogen.) Some oestradiol is good for men because it supports bone density and even men can get osteoporosis but too much leads to erectile dysfunction and man boobs, as well as increases risks of BPH. (Benign prostatic hyperplasia or enlarged prostate).

An interesting snippet to note: If you feel your testosterone levels are dropping, just having a testosterone injection may NOT benefit you at all. Particularly if your aromatase enzymes are elevated. More testosterone and lots of aromatase will just make more oestrogen, which will make the situation worse.

Often a dead giveaway as to whether you have higher levels of oestrogen is low energy, low motivation, low libido, and a big belly. Consult with a doctor who specialises in male hormones, or a Functional medicine practitioner if you suspect any of these symptoms may be a problem but, in the meantime, the following will help inhibit aromatase.

- Fibre
- Flaxseed

- Chrysin
- Green tea
- Stinging nettle (don't chew this directly)
- Zinc
- Vitamin C
- Lose belly fat.
- Stress levels. (Discussed in more detail later on) Pregnenalone (from cholesterol and the building block for testosterone) also makes progesterone (mistakenly called a female hormone) and progesterone is important to make cortisol (and a bit of testosterone as well). If you are very stressed, the body will take as much pregnenalone as it needs to make cortisol, which will leave little left over for testosterone production. This is why stress may affect your ability to get or maintain an erection.
- Alcohol and smoking both lower testosterone.

Activity: Add more zinc-rich foods to your diet to support free testosterone. E.g., Oysters, beef steak, pumpkin seeds, cashew nuts and chickpeas are all high in zinc.

Men also secrete progesterone, oestrogen, and that all-important oxytocin. As With women, progesterone in men is very useful. Firstly, as mentioned, progesterone is the precursor, or building block for cortisol, so when you are working long hours at the office to finish that project and your stress levels are rising, then the cortisol your body needs to help you cope, comes from progesterone. Plus, progesterone is anti-estrogenic. It opposes oestrogen and oestrogen levels rise in direct proportion to the growing belly as you get older. High oestrogen is also the wicked witch that increases your risks of BPH (benign prostatic hyperplasia) when your prostate enlarges, and you feel the need to get up four times a night to wee out 3 drops.

Chemicals such as BPA and pesticides, and other endocrine disrupting chemicals, also stimulate the formation of oestrogen and oestrogen inhibits testosterone. A definite negative feedback loop for virility.

Keen to make babies? If you are wanting to increase fertility and get those little swimmers at their best, here are a few factors that affect fertility.

- Obesity
- Smoking
- Alcohol
- Heavy metals (do you have silver amalgam in your teeth?)
- Some other drugs: i.e., marijuana, cocaine, some antihypertensives, methotrexate and others. If you are on medication, read the package insert or ask Dr Google.
- Environmental toxins and chemical such as phthalates (really, I didn't make this word up) BPA (Avoid drinking from plastic) and pesticides.

What about **oxytocin**? This is a wonderful bonding hormone. It helps you feel love and connection and when you cuddle, or play, oxytocin is released, which makes you feel connected and more loving towards your partner and want to cuddle more and so on. Naturally stress kills oxytocin but even coming home and playing with your dog for a bit, can help release this love hormone.

Cortisol deserves special mention here. When we are stressed, our body releases adrenalin, which is good for that moment, but whenever adrenalin is released, the body also releases cortisol. Cortisol is an anti-inflammatory and it 'cools' the adrenalin response. This sounds like a good thing, and it is, but only for short moments. Prolonged stress leads to a constant 'fight or flight' state where cortisol is always being released. The result of this is increased belly fat because cortisol, in its clever way, triggers the release of stored sugar from the liver and the muscles. This is because the body thinks it may need to run away. The body cannot distinguish the difference between an angry Sabre tooth tiger and a very annoying and demanding boss. Both trigger the fight or flight response and the release of adrenalin and cortisol. If the body does need to run, it will need fuel to do this, so cortisol makes sure it gets the fuel by triggering the release from your liver and muscles. Basically, when you are stressed, you are eating all the time without the enjoyment of tasting the food and the result of all this eating is we get fat.

Insulin. This section would not be complete if I didn't mention insulin. Insulin is a hormone that tells the body to store energy. When your body is exposed to too much insulin, either with a very high carbohydrate diet, or too many meals in the day or when you are nibbling all the time, (if we ate poor nutrient dense grass we might need to 'graze', but we don't. Our grazing takes the form of very high caloric, often sugar - laden foods or cool drinks) the cells eventually become desensitized to insulin. A bit like your ears when you are asked repeatedly to take out the trash…they go into selective hearing. We call this 'insulin resistance' and it has a profoundly negative effect on the secretion of testosterone. This is one of the important reasons to try and lose that gut…. but more on this important tip later.

Activity: The best blanket suggestions for properly balance hormones is:

- Address your stress
- Lose weight
- Give up smoking

Is my body managing my stress?

Whether young or old, cortisol and our ability to manage stress, is the cornerstone of balanced hormones. It affects our sleep patterns, our rate of healing and even our immune function and the domino effect is extensive. High cortisol (an adaptive response when we are under stress), or depleted cortisol (when we have been under stress for too long), both have a negative ripple effect on all the other hormones. The HPA axis: the hypothalamus-pituitary-adrenal axis, as well as the HPT axis: the hypothalamus-pituitary-thyroid axis, are both stabilising columns in our sense of wellbeing as we age. Any imbalance will, as with a building, topple the whole structure.

The link to sexual prowess: If pregnenalone is a building block for testosterone as well as a building block for cortisol, and stress requires cortisol to manage it, then does stress impact on my production of testosterone?

There is a process that has been named 'pregnenolone steal' that plays a role here.

Perhaps you are madly busy at work, but you seem to be managing your work schedule well. You have an intense exercise regime over the weekend, also completed and enjoyed but your libido is falling off and you are just tired and dispirited. Is your body actually managing the stress adequately? What are the signs to look out for to measure this?

- Morning fatigue – You really need that caffeine hit.
- An energy dip from about 2pm-4pm, where you need more coffee to pull you through.
- A second wind at around 6pm and then another little slump after dinner while you have a short snooze in front of the TV
- Another "Second wind" at 11 p.m. that lasts until after midnight, when you finally go to sleep.
- Cravings for foods high in salt and fat
- Mild depression or a flat feeling.
- Lack of energy
- You notice you are not as strong as you were when you work out.

- Orthostatic hypotension. You feel lightheaded if you get up too quickly from the couch.
- Decreased sex drive
- You catch yourself sighing a lot

The body responds to managing stress in the same way it responds to a threat against your life. Managing stress is actually a survival mechanism. In other words, the body prioritizes this to keep you alive, so it will take as much pregnenolone as it needs to make as much cortisol as it needs. When you are stressed, very low on the list is making babies so if you are highly stressed, this may result in nearly all the pregnenalone being stolen from the hormones to make cortisol. The result is…. Lower testosterone and possibly erectile dysfunction.

Additionally, a high stress level can be very damaging to health and not just to your sex drive and consequently, your ability to perform. It also increases your risk of having a heart attack, increased hypertension, and a stroke. It is not a luxury to take time off. Spending time doing NOTHING is essential for men. (Show this to your partner when you are having a 'do nothing' moment).

Fortunately, stress is also resolved by; receiving your own massages; (receiving pelvic massages taught in the female version of this book) going on easy, relaxing walks with your partner or even the dog; watching comedies on television and engaging in a hobby you love to do.

Go on a media holiday for a while. Avoid the news and avoid people who drain your energy and make demands on your life. We all need a break every so often and taking a health break is important for longevity as well as sensual and sexual pleasure.

I cannot emphasize enough though, that stress is a major de-stabiliser, and taking 'me -time' is not a luxury but an essential part of being well and feeling good. I think the reasons people don't address stress is that firstly, many of the causes of stress just don't (or can't) go away and because we cannot remove the cause, we believe that stress will be a part of our lives as long as the stressor is there, and secondly, the ways to address stress seem so nebulous. A massage, for goodness sake! I don't have time for that and how is that going to make a difference? But trust me. A massage, or any other stress reliever, will reduce cortisol. Even taking some deep breaths lowers the adrenalin hit.

Activity: Avoid the news for a few days and use that time to play with your kids or open a loving conversation with your partner.

Losing the belly to gain the testosterone benefit. Your least favourite info day.

Yes, yes, yes, I can hear you say. I know I need to lose my belly fat, but it isn't as easy as all that. Plus, because women are very forgiving and they seldom moan at their men about their love handles, it is easy to dismiss them as unimportant. But are they?

Belly fat is where men load on the weight. Even otherwise trim men can sometimes have a small paunch. Is it even important to bother about then?

Well, often life gets away from us and what starts off as something barely noticeable creeps up until when you look again, you cannot see your penis. Belly fat is like a thermometer for poor health. It is often the first outward manifestation of an inner imbalance and because it is first, if you see it approaching, and catch it early, the cascade of benefits leaks into other areas of a soon- to- be healthy body.

Aside from needing to reposition yourself during sex so you don't crush the woman you are on top of, what does belly fat represent?

Associated with insulin resistance, it is also a reflection of visceral fat. In other words, the bigger the belly, the more fat encases the organs like the heart. Plus, fat on the belly may also reflect a fatty liver. There is a close association between a condition called non-alcoholic fatty liver disease and insulin resistance and both have a negative impact in the body.

Getting rid of body fat for a man is generally a much easier process than it is for a woman. Many women start a program with their partner and for every 0.5gm she loses, he manages to lose 2kg. What amazes me is that these men remain alive and are not repeatedly stabbed in the eye by their starved and miserably hungry partners.

For those men who want to address their belly fat, here is the way to start.

Reduce insulin exposure in your body. This means cut down on, or better still, cut out, high- carbohydrate foods such as bread, pasta, potato, and beer. (Sorry guys).

Do not snack. Every time we eat our body will release insulin in response to the food we take in. Eating food, even small amounts of low-calorie food, will release insulin and as I said before, insulin is a hormone that tells the body to store energy. We want times when there is NO insulin in our body. Go 4-5 hours between meals when you eat nothing at all. No milk in your tea and no food. Not even that tiny biscotti that accompanies your black coffee. Water and herbal tea though, are fine.

Stop eating 3 hours before you go to bed and do not eat even a tiny almond, let alone a savory cheese straw, before you go to sleep. Eating before bed messes with both insulin and leptin and you will not lose weight that way.

Practice intermittent fasting. This is, without a doubt, the most fantastic way to normalize insulin and lose weight AND done well, it does allow one to enjoy a glass of wine with dinner. How does one intermittent fast? It is so easy. The plan is to go around 14-16 hours with no food (only water, black coffee, or herbal tea) and what better time to do this than when we are sleeping. So, let's say you finish dinner at 8pm. You go to bed at around 10.30 and asleep by 11. To go 14-16 hours no food means that when you wake up, you will not eat (you may have black coffee with xylitol or erythritol) until between 10am and midday, at which time you may enjoy your delicious lunch. It may take you a while to get into this. If you are badly insulin resistant you will most probably not manage to go long in between meals but a little tip here: if you are starving, EAT, but the next day, eat more fat and protein at the meal before starvation set in. Slowly the body becomes more efficient at burning stored fat and you will manage the longer times between meals.

Glucagon vs Insulin. If insulin is the hormone that tells the body to store energy, glucagon is the hormone that tells the body to burn energy. Both come from the pancreas, but the pancreas will only secrete one at a time. If you have eaten carbs and the pancreas is secreting insulin, it will hold off on the glucagon, but when you take breaks between meals, the pancreas secretes glucagon and this triggers fat burning in the body. Bye bye belly fat.

The benefits of the diminishing belly will be:
- Decreased oestrogen exposure
- Decreased aromatase
- Decreased risk of heart attack and stroke

- Decreased inflammation. (Fat is very inflammatory
- Increased testosterone
- Increased energy
- A new view of your penis.

Activity. Avoid any snacking after dinner and try and eat your last meal 3 hours before you go to bed.

Filling in some gaps: A hormone and weight loss review

There are many hormones and other chemicals that affect how we feel on a daily basis and certainly, how we feel affects whether or not we either want to, or have the energy to, have sex, or even masturbate.

The biggest impactors are:
- Insulin
- Cortisol (always)
- Sex hormones (oestrogen, progesterone, testosterone)
- Thyroid hormones. Even men have thyroid problems
- Other metabolic (how we process our food for energy) hormones. i.e., Leptin, ghrelin
- Losing the paunch

Unlike women, men are not so hard on themselves when they carry a bit of extra weight but the health impact on the body, as well as on sexual performance, may kick you into action. You have seen how stress affects weight, as well as the quality of your erection, but excess weight also has a creeping influence on our sense of buoyancy and our light-hearted playfulness. Important when it comes to impressing the chicks. Specifically, excess weight and the insulin resistance that a belly augurs, cause an excess of inflammatory cytokines (more hormones) and these inflammatory messengers affect out brain neurotransmitters such as serotonin and dopamine, and lead to depression and lack of motivation. It's such a dual kick in the pants because low testosterone also leads to low motivation. Hard to want to be a marathon stud in bed when the armchair and Netflix are just so much more appealing.

What if the creeping belly is no longer so creeping? Losing it is the start towards rekindling desire and not only outstanding performance but mind-blowing pleasure. Insulin is the first recalcitrant hormone to get into check in order to lose the belly but there are others:

1.   Leptin

Leptin impacts on all the other hormones responsible for weight loss and general health. Leptin is produced by fat cells and the more fat we have; the more leptin is produced. The importance of this is that leptin informs the brain (hormone messenger) how much fat we are carrying, and the brain will then either stimulate or suppress appetite accordingly, as well as increase or decrease basal metabolism. (Through the thyroid gland). The higher the fat levels, the higher the leptin, the faster the metabolism and the lower the appetite. Hooray!

Specifically, if we gain weight, leptin increases, and the desire to eat is suppressed, as well as energy expenditure increased. (Metabolic rate rises). But too much fat creates a leptin resistance similar to insulin resistance. The result of this is the message leptin is trying to convey to the brain, to reduce our appetite, is simply not getting through and our appetite remains high, despite sufficient fat.

 Conversely, as weight is lost (too fast) and fat cells begin to decrease, leptin will tell the body there is potential famine coming and appetite will increase, and metabolism will decrease (Leptin informs thyroid hormones to step down their cellular energy expenditure levels) in order to hold on the present amount of stored energy.

2. Ghrelin

Ghrelin is a short acting hormone, produced in the stomach, which sends a signal of hunger when it is time for us to eat. It works together with leptin to regulate your appetite.

Once you eat food, ghrelin secretion stops. This is a fine co- ordinated dance. If there is an imbalance, it doesn't matter how much will- power you may have, dieting will be extremely difficult.

Too much leptin will result in resistance to the message of 'decrease appetite' and too much ghrelin will lead to a person overeating. The two together "conspire" to keep you fat.

High carbohydrate diets not only spike your insulin but cause a rise in ghrelin.

What can I do?

If you are paying particular attention to this section, chances are you failed the 'dick test' and no matter how far forward you crane your neck, you cannot see your dick, let alone feel comfortable about clipping the hair short with dangerous scissors, all by feel alone. In this case, being patient is very valuable because no matter what miracle diet, supplement, or injection you go on, it will take time for the body to balance the leptin, insulin, and ghrelin.

- Be patient!
- Do not radically cut calorie intake. Go slow.
- Eat enough to satisfy basal metabolic needs. Your heart and brain need some energy too.
- Eat highly nutritious food to keep vitamins and mineral levels high. Lots of veggies.
- Eat 2-3 times a day, not 5, to keep insulin levels down.
- Cut out all processed carbohydrates that spike insulin. Avoid fruit juice and fizzy cans.
- Eat foods that feed the body. No empty calories.
- Eat protein with every meal to slow insulin release.
- No snacking.
- Add exercise: even gentle walking every day. Exercise lowers leptin levels as well as increasing energy demands.
- Occasionally fast for 24hours. Fasting lowers leptin levels and pulls down insulin.
- Balance eating to minimize leptin and insulin resistance.
- Develop better sleep patterns to reduce stress. Sleep 7-8 hours a night.
- Avoid surgery such as gastric bypass. Gastric bypass lowers the levels of ghrelin because there are fewer stomach cells that can manufacture it.
- Supplements such as acetyl- L-carnitine and omega 3 also contribute to balancing growth hormone and leptin.

Activity: Add intermittent fasting as the most impactful weight-loss activity.

Curtail snippiness and be calm and accessible to your woman

Being snippy and irritable will not only make you unpleasant to be with and will NOT get you laid, but when you are feeling low and depressed your desire for sex diminishes as well so you may not care. Depression used to be more of a woman's problem but no more. Nowadays more men are feeling depressed more frequently and because men generally tend not to ask for help and support as frequently as women, and, unlike women, may not have the types of relationships with their friends where they can say… 'I am feeling a bit low', men may feel left out in the cold and isolated.

Low mood and depression.

With the high pace at which many of us are forced to run our lives, the poor-quality fast foods we eat and the exposure to xenoestrogens that increase the level of oestrogen in the blood, men are experiencing mood swings and depression. Men have to deal with a lot. They feel responsible for the safety and security of their family and may be in either physically or mentally demanding jobs with no relief. Sleep becomes elusive and in fact, men tend to self-medicate with alcohol and recreational drugs more than women when they need to relax and yet cannot. Plus, certain gene SNPs (discussed soon) may predispose men to an inability to relax and thus open up the door to addictive habits, as they try and moderate the demands by using alcohol to try and relax.

Low motivation, depression, anxiety, and low self-esteem may rear their ugly heads. Even when the sky is blue, your family is safe and happy and your relationship is stable, you may be unable to get out of the pit.

When something is not right the symptoms may include:

- Restless sleep or insomnia
- Occasionally oversleeping
- Energy slumps
- Loss of appetite or need to eat voraciously
- Loss of libido
- Restlessness
- Brain fog

- Feelings of worthlessness or guilt
- Thoughts about dying or suicide
- Lack of motivation or interest in life activities

Depression is more complex than simply taking an antidepressant will solve. In fact, while serotonin imbalance is mostly touted as being the cause of depression, inflammation is showing its ugly head (pardon the pun) as a real influence on depression. A new field called 'Immuno-Neurology' is addressing the association between inflammation and depression, with some interesting results. In the meantime, understanding inflammation in our body and taking steps to reduce it, may also put us over the threshold in managing our depression and low mood.

Watch out for inflammatory triggers

- 80 % of our serotonin is manufactured in the gut and a healthy gut is a great place to start.
- Avoid sugar. The flood of insulin that accompanies sugar (and starchy carbohydrate) intake is extremely inflammatory and there are insulin receptors in the brain that are affected by this.
- Repeated exposure to chemicals such as pesticides, and hormone disrupters, will also increase inflammation in our body.
- Gluten and dairy, particularly in sensitive individuals, keeps our immune response alert, and with it, our inflammatory response because the two go hand in hand.
- Exposure to pathogens and parasites. Often these are not overt. We struggle with fatigue, gut disturbances, headaches, and other non-specific indications that we may be infected with pathogens. Our immune system (together with our inflammatory system) remains on high alert as long as we harbour unwanted organisms.
- Chronic stress. This may be perceived stress from our workplace or perhaps a family relationship, or physical stress brought on by infections, food sensitivities, high sugar intake or disease.

What can we do to reduce the impact and be ready for more relaxed and satisfying sex?

Address your stress. Remove the stress effect of gluten, sugar and dairy and add calming activities such as a walk or time spent pottering around the garage. A pelvic massage from a loving woman will do wonders. (I promise I tell her how in her book)

Increase your exercise. If you are very busy then a 30 second quick burst of high intensity running on the spot or dash up and down the stairs at work to get your heart rate elevated, will work well. Try and do this several times a day. See information on exercise for the rushed man coming up soon

Consider adding a daily probiotic. The anti-inflammatory effect of certain good probiotics can be very beneficial in reducing inflammation. Remember to go very slow. Certain people do not deal well with, and become sniffly, when adding a probiotic because probiotics are high in histamine. In this case you may tolerate fermented foods better.

Practice good sleep habits. This may seem a rather odd suggestion for reducing inflammation, but chronic exhaustion is inflammation promoting. Allow for 8 hours of sleep. Sleep in a completely dark room and avoid using any gadget that emits blue light an hour or two before bed. Alternatively wear yellow glasses from the time the outside light begins to drop, to cut the blue light. Cool movie star look, or just be ok with being the butt of family jokes.

Activity: Add a good probiotic on a daily basis to normalise the microbiome.

Medications and deficiencies that trigger depression, low libido, and erectile dysfunction.

Firstly, there is much in the literature about low magnesium and its association with depression. In fact, magnesium is a mineral with wonderful health benefits. In the brain, when magnesium is low, the requirements for neuronal health are not met and the result is nerve damage, which may cause depression. Plus, to make serotonin, (and dopamine and adrenalin) the body needs... you guessed it... Magnesium. (as well as vitamin B's). As our standard diet is generally low in magnesium, a high proportion of the population is magnesium deficient, and this has a cascade effect on mental well- being as well.

In addition to poor magnesium intake, many medications rob the body of magnesium. For example:

- Diuretics
- Anti-inflammatories, some antihistamines, and some anti-biotics
- Aspirin
- Insulin
- Chemotherapy treatment
- Proton pump inhibiters
- Antacids
- High doses of calcium
- Coffee
- Ritalin

Vitamin B12 is another essential vitamin for brain health. As with the onset of apparent Alzheimer's symptoms, depression may also arise with low B12. Metformin for diabetics, gout medication, and many antibiotics all deplete vitamin B12.

In addition: Drugs that may directly cause depression.

- Accutane (Acne)
- Beta blockers (High blood pressure)
- Contraceptives
- Cortico-steroids (anti-inflammatory)

What about medications that rob you of your libido or cause erectile dysfunction?

- There are quite a few so if you are struggling with erectile dysfunction or loss of libido and are on prescription drugs, check the package insert and talk to your doctor about an alternative. The list includes
- Diuretics and high- blood- pressure drugs
- Antidepressants
- Antihistamines
- Non-steroidal anti-inflammatory drugs. (Sometimes taken for sporting injuries or arthritis).
- Muscle relaxants. (Mm… too much relaxant clearly)
- Parkinson's medication
- Chemotherapy drugs
- Amphetamines
- Nicotine
- Opiates

Sometimes ED is not mentioned as a side effect on the package insert but many of these drugs affect blood vessels, sometimes permanently, so do your own research.

Activity: Take stock of prescription medication you are on and research side effects.

Some info on genes. (Not juicy stuff so skip if you don't care!)

Why is my response to health, energy, vitality, and sexuality different to my best mate?

Genes are the blueprint that we inherit from our parents. They determine whether we have brown hair or blue eyes. That genetic determination is immutable, but when it comes to health and even sexuality, genetic influences are not cast in stone.

Genes are responsible for creating every protein that builds the cells and organs in our body, and for every enzyme used in chemical reactions and for every hormone involved in cellular communication. They are important for what hormones we make but also what hormones we get rid of after we have finished with them. In a practical example: If excess oestrogen may give you man- boobs and erectile dysfunction, what role do your genes play of your body holding on to too much oestrogen?

 If our genes become damaged in some way, our body can no longer use a perfect pattern for making perfect hormones, enzymes, and necessary proteins; that is, if the genetic pattern is damaged, the result will be sub-optimal. That doesn't necessarily mean that a protein created from a damaged gene won't work at all, it just means that it won't work as well.

Humans have inherited around 25,000 different gene sequences. These sequences or 'chains' the pattern to make different proteins. However, as part of our genetic make-up we also inherit thousands of different SNPs. 'SNP' stands for 'single nucleotide polymorphism', which means that a gene sequence has a single variation in the sequence. There are millions of SNPs in the human genome (the genome being all our hereditary information encoded in our DNA).

What this means for you and me is that there are many opportunities for tiny variations in our cells, enzymes and hormones that may result in variations in our inherited genetic make-up.

These variations impact on things like our ability to detoxify, our risk of cancer, our oxidation capacity, and many others. SNPs are the reason that there is no such thing as one-size-fits-all when it comes to health.

The wonderful fact about genes is that your thoughts, your environment, your food, your stress levels, and your exercise patterns—all of which we have some control over—have profound influence over the expression of almost all our genes.

 The science of epigenetics studies how the environment affects the expression of our genes. (In other words, which genes will be 'turned on' and which genes will remain unexpressed). So, with a certain amount of influence, we are at the helm of our genetic expression.

Certainly, there are genes that predispose towards risky conditions such as diabetes or even obesity but carrying such a gene is not enough to result in the actual manifestation of the illness—the gene still must be expressed or turned on. However, because we may not know about the factors that influence gene expression, we may make mistakes that turn on the wrong genes or even turn off the right ones.

What is important to know is that we are not helpless in the face of our genetic inheritance: we can affect what plays out in our body.

What gene SNPs may mess with your hormone balance and lead to man- boobs, prostate cancer, or erectile dysfunction?

A gene profile has lots of valuable information but understanding it and putting it into context it is a complex process and requires interpretation by a practitioner knowledgeable about gene SNP's but in short:

Oestrogen: You have seen from a few days ago that excess oestrogen has some unfortunate effects in the male body but why would you, as a male, have too much oestrogen anyway? Normally the body is adept at keeping the balance needed to hold what's important and dump what isn't, but other factors may influence this process.

We all have metabolic enzymes, manufactured in the liver, that act on our hormones and in the case of oestrogen, turn estrogen into forms (metabolites) that have higher risks than other metabolites. Depending on our inherited SNP's (remember those variations in the gene that we all have?), our levels of these risky metabolites may be higher or lower.

When estrogen is metabolised in the body, one of the processes is called 'hydroxylation' and it is this 'hydroxylated estrogen' that may turn estrogen into a damaging, cancer promoting, penis-wilting form, depending on what particular enzyme acts on the estrogen.

The enzymes that trigger the hydroxylation process are called Cytochrome P450's (CYP 450's) We all have them, and they are essential for detoxification. These CYP450's are also involved in detoxifying drugs and chemicals.

 If we have SNPs in the genes coding for these particular enzymes, the body makes a small error in making the enzyme, resulting in potentially more risky estrogen metabolites. These SNPs can be measured and if there is a history of breast or prostate cancer, then a gene profile may be advisable.

What SNP's are associated with estrogen metabolism?

CYP1B1: This enzyme forms 4 hydroxy- estrone and 4 hydroxy- oestradiol, - unstable and risky oestrogen metabolites that form semiquinones, which damage DNA, thus increasing the risk of breast and prostate cancer. A SNP in 1B1 increases the formation of these risky 4Hydroxy 'oestrogens'.

If you have this SNP, in order to slow this process down and thus form less of these 1B1 metabolites, the following nutrients can be helpful: Grapefruit, (remember some pharmaceuticals are also metabolised via 1B1, so slowing it down may result in an excess of the pharmaceutical drug remaining for longer in the body), citrus peel and flax seeds.

CYP3A4: Forms 16-alpha hydroxy- estrone, considered also to be risky. A SNP in 3A4 speeds up the formation of these 16-alpha hydroxy's and therefore may result in an increase in cancer risk. Slowing 3A4 may mitigate this risk. CYP 3A4 has been implicated in the development of prostate cancer due to its oxidative deactivation of testosterone. Nutrients that slow 3A4 are grapefruit again, pomegranate, peppermint, and liquorice.

CYP1A1: This enzyme forms metabolites called 2- hydroxy- estrone and 2 - hydroxy- oestradiol. Unlike the other forms, this metabolite is considered to be protective of breast tissue (yup, men also get breast cancer) and prostate cancer, thus an activation of this enzyme may reduce your risk of both breast and prostate cancer. Also, unlike the other 2, a SNP in this gene slows down the formation of the more protective 2 hydroxy's and thus needs to be stimulated. DIM (diindolylmethane…huh?) and berries such as blackberries and blueberries, will upregulate (speed up) 1A1.

COMT: (catechol oxygen methyltransferase). This is a very important enzyme in the detoxification of oestrogen. A SNP in this enzyme significantly slows the clearance of oestrogen, thus increasing the time of oestrogen exposure, which has long been considered a risk factor in breast cancer. In addition, BPA slows COMT even more, as does stress, mercury, high homocysteine, and green tea; EGCG (an example of a generally considered beneficial nutrient that may not benefit everyone). Support COMT with magnesium and methyl B vitamins. Plus, this SNP is also involved in the detoxification and clearance of adrenalin. A slow clearance of adrenalin may lead to sleep problems and inability to relax. This impacts heavily on the ability to manage stress and you have heard me harp on about how important it is to reduce stress for a happy time in the bedroom.

Activity. Investigate what gene profiling is available in your country. 23andme has a comprehensive one but it will require interpretation by a practitioner knowledgeable about gene SNPs

Putting it all together. A short overview of signs you may have a hormone imbalance.

Sometimes your wives may start to notice and comment that you have 'changed'. These changes may reflect hormonal changes

As men age, they may experience the following symptoms and with the ubiquitous poor diet and high stress levels, men may even begin experiencing symptoms in their late 30's. Factors such as age, stress levels, belly fat, alcohol intake and medication, all conspire to influence how you feel, both physically as well as mentally and emotionally.

Signs of hormone imbalance may include:
- Increased belly fat
- Loss of or diminished libido
- Erectile dysfunction
- Decreased muscle mass and strength
- Loss of head hair
- Prostate problems
- Insomnia
- Depression
- Irritability

First step would be to get the levels tested properly. Often clinics that specialise in male sexual health are the best option for comprehensive testing and evaluation.

Tests should include:
- Cortisol
- DHEA-S
- Dihydrotestosterone (DHT)
- Androstenedione
- Progesterone
- Estrone
- A gene profile

Men also have progesterone and estrogen, and low levels of progesterone (for men) may contribute to aggression and irritability and high levels of estrogen (for men) affect belly fat as well as risk of prostate cancer.

 As mentioned, men with high levels of aromatase more readily convert testosterone into oestrogen and this will affect libido, motivation, physical strength as well as mood. Plus, too much oestrogen in men increases the risk of prostate cancer.

Gene testing, where the gene SNPs mentioned earlier, such as CYP 1B1 and COMT, are present, influence the oestrogen metabolites retained in the body, and these may not only affect risk of breast cancer, (yes, even with men) but also prostate cancer risk. Clearing oestrogen (or not making too much to begin with) is just as important for men as it is for women.

This is not a linear process which is why thinking that a single prescription item, or just a few supplements will make any difference at all, is a useless process. The process of good health and happy sex is multi-dimensional but each step along the line is within your control.

In my opinion though, first on the list in addressing hormonal imbalance, is for men to lose that belly.   Did I say that already?

Activity: See your doctor about getting some baseline hormone tests.

Hair loss deserves special mention. Even though generally women don't care.

I suspect many men view creeping hair loss the same way women view creeping belly fat; With total horror and in both cases, a sense of helplessness resounds. So, what happens to the head hair follicles on men that cause them to drop hair?

It is all the fault of an enzyme called 5 -alpha reductase that converts testosterone to DHT, dihydrotestosterone. DHT is a testosterone metabolite that is even more potent than testosterone. Does this sound like a good thing? Well, in excess, it's not. DHT is found in prostate tissue and contributes to benign prostatic hypertrophy, where the prostate grows and starts causing problems in urination in older men: Plus, DHT is associated with male pattern baldness. When the enzyme 5-alphareductase is up-regulated, then more DHT is produced, and the side effects get worse.

Certain triggers for a more active 5-alphareductase include:
- Obesity (Again)
- Insulin resistance
- Type II diabetes

What can be done to inhibit this problematic enzyme?
- Lose that belly (nag nag…typical woman)
- Saw Palmetto (serenoarepens)
- Nettles (*Urticadioica*)
- Finasteride (from your doctor)
- Progesterone (from your doctor)

Dietary additions
- EGCG: from green tea. Watch out if you are someone who cannot sleep.
- Lycopene inhibits 5-alpha so eat tomato, carrots, watermelon, and mango
- L-Lysine: from nuts such as almonds and walnuts

- Zinc: from spinach and kale (also good for clearing excess oestrogen) but be careful if you suffer from gout. Spinach is high in purines so bad for gout.
- Delta-7 stearine: from pumpkin seeds (helps to clear the DHT from the hair follicle).

Activity: Double check you have included some zinc rich foods in your diet.

Stress in more detail. Pregnenolone Steal.

You have already been introduced to this concept but it's important, so here it is again.

Pregnenolone (different from Progesterone) is a rather fabulous hormone. Actually, it is the mother to all our hormones and as a mother, needs some potency and power to ensure all her baby hormones are properly cared for. As the mother hormone, Pregnenolone has some remarkable benefits such as:

- Anti -ageing
- Stress management
- Mental acuity
- Energy support
- Anti-depressant

A deficiency in Pregnenolone will impact on the efficacy of ALL other hormones. Similarly, if one of the baby hormones, (cortisol) hogs all the mother Pregnenolone, then the other babies will suffer.

I keep harping on about stress and here is another example of the insidious and damaging effect of stress. When we are under stress, and cortisol is released from our adrenals to 'cool' the body and manage the deleterious effects, pregnenolone, our mother hormone, is the precursor. In other words, the foundational building block that our body uses to create the cortisol. The more cortisol that is required when we experience chronic, never-ending stress, the more pregnenolone building blocks are required. Makes sense, doesn't it?

However, imagine we have to build a house and we have a pile of bricks (Pregnenolone), but part of the house is on boggy ground and the bricks start to sink, so we madly supply bricks from our pile for that boggy area, depleting the pile so the rest of the house gets built at a slower rate, or even not at all. That's what happens here. Pregnenolone (amongst other complex factors) ALSO supplies building material for our other hormones, namely progesterone and DHEA (that makes our testosterone and oestrogen). So now progesterone, testosterone and oestrogen slow to a snail's pace because all the pregnenolone is going to make cortisol. We call this Pregnenolone

Steal and the solution is to resolve the stress, reduce the cortisol demand and free up the pregnenolone. In situations of unavoidable stress, it is possible to get pregnenolone as a supplement, but you would need to speak to your doctor about that. It is available only through special compounding pharmacies.

Activity: Make a conscious effort to have breathing sessions throughout the day. Set a ping on your phone and just breathe deeply for 3o seconds when the phone pings.

Many men are very sporty and very active but occasionally, life slowly squeezes the time available to partake in a sport you enjoy, or even a workout at the gym, into a smaller and more infrequent time frame. We know exercise is important and I would wager that when you do have time, you feel better as a result but what if you simply do not get the time? In this situation Tabata training is a godsend.

What is Tabata Training?

Tabata is a form of high intensity interval training that brings very good results and fantastic benefits with a short but intense training period only 2-3 times a week. Depending on your choice of exercise during your Tabata, you may still build muscle and there are lots of wonderful combinations with trainers on the internet. Not only does Tabata maximizes fat burning, it also increases the release of human growth hormone. Great for maintaining dense muscles. It has the added benefit of burning more calories overall than other forms of exercise because, provided you do not eat directly after the Tabata, your body will continue to burn fat even after you finish training. On top of that, if you do it properly, it only takes 4 minutes of actual high intensity training. With a warmup of 2-3 minutes, your total session takes less than 10 minutes. This may be perfect for the average busy executive who has little free time.

However, it is extreme and should be by no means easy. If it is easy, then you are not doing it properly. It is self-limiting because you can work at your own level of fitness and your own pace so even people who are unfit can do Tabata training because the goal is to get 'your' heart rate high. What is a fast pace for you, may be a slower pace for someone else but as you get fitter, you will go faster and harder, so the body sets its own limits.

How?

Find an aerobic (cardiac) activity, or a hybrid activity using light enough weights to move fast without hurting yourself. Choose an activity where you can go as fast as possible and then transition to slow without using precious minutes to slow down.

- Running
- Swimming
- Cycling
- Stationary bike
- Burpees
- Star jumps
- Skipping
- Rowing
- Working with small weights or ropes.

Warm up by doing the activity at a moderate pace for a few minutes.

Go as fast as you possibly can for 20 seconds and then slow for 10 seconds.

Repeat this cycle for a total of 8 altogether.

For this to work properly, from about cycle 5- 8 you should be really out of breath.

Benefits.
- Increase anaerobic capacity
- Increase aerobic capacity
- Increase VO2 max.
- Increase production of Mitochondria (little energy producing cells in your body)
- Decrease fasting Insulin
- Decrease abdominal fat
- Increase heart rate

Activity: Set a schedule on your phone for a 5- minute gap, three times a week, to practice Tabata. Preferably not just before bed.

Conclusion

Making changes is never easy and often the desirable end result seems too far away to justify the effort, but taking a small step, even only one a week, will slowly and inexorably take you to your goal. Maximizing your masculinity is the essence of who you are, to your core, and well worth the effort. Not only will you feel stronger, more resilient, sexier, but this will spill over into how women see you and want to interact with you.

To dive deeper into what women want when you are with them, both in the bedroom and in your interactions and conversation, take a look at, 'Ignite Her Fire', for a detailed roadmap.

Have fun with the information offered in this book and I would love to hear about your successes.

Well done and chat soon

Maxine

- Lose the belly fat
- Have your cholesterol checked if you have lost your libido
- Reduce insulin by avoiding processed foods and bread, pasta, potato, and rice
- Reduce your stress. This is extremely important.
- Go on relaxing walks
- Have regular massages
- Practice deep breathing several times a day
- Take quiet time; Perhaps meditate or listen to music
- Give up smoking
- Reduce alcohol intake
- If you are on medication, google the side effects
- Avoid drinking out of plastic bottles; Use glass
- Limit coffee to not more than 2 cups per day
- Reduce Belly fat to achieve the following
- Decrease oestrogen
- Reduce risk of visceral fat
- Reduce risk of NAFLD
- Support belly fat loss by the following suggestions
  - No snacking
  - Reduce carbohydrate intake
  - Intermittent fasting
  - Last meal 3 hours before bed
  - Eat nutrient dense food
  - Avoid processed food
- Have a hormone panel test
- Test your HBA1c and fasting insulin
- Consult with a nutritionist or functional medicine practitioner
- Address your sleep patterns by:
  - Wearing yellow glasses in the evening to cut blue light
  - Installing a blue light filter on your phone and computer
  - Using and eye mask
  - Installing blackout curtains
- Get help if you feel low and depressed
- Keep systemic inflammation low by
  - Avoiding sugar
  - Detoxing from heavy metals and other chemicals

- o   Avoiding gluten and dairy
- Check for systemic parasites
- Reduce stress
- Address your gut health to support serotonin production
- Add some form of exercise into your day… even just 5 minutes of Tabata
- Gain control of the small messes in your life, even if just tidying your room
- If you have a partner, add special things to do for her or with her, at random days in your diary. Prepare the whole year in advance. You can even shop for non-perishables in advance for those emergency appreciation moments.
- Choose not to be offended, bitter or angry about past events. The past is over. Why would you want to bring such negativity into your future
- Congratulate yourself on a job well done and resolve to keep growing

In vitality and joy

Maxine

ABOUT THE AUTHOR

Jules Allen-Rowland, a Functional Medicine Practitioner, writes under the pseudonym Maxine Gregg in the Xpert range. In practice for more than 15 years and with a bachelor's degree in psychology and communication, certified in health, nutrition, and exercise science, as well as her FM qualification, Jules has worked with more than two thousand patients, young and old. Many of these patients have hormonal and mood imbalances that have led to less-than-satisfying sex lives, and many expressed a wish for a user-friendly solution.

Starting the Xpert range is a step towards that solution and has allowed Jules to use her knowledge as a Functional Medicine Practitioner to address serious lifestyle issues in a light-hearted way, removing the 'weight of change' with regard to health challenges and make them fun and do-able, without compromising the information needed to enjoy lives of vitality and joy.

Other books in the Xpert range include:

Ignite Her Fire: B08FZS4ZF5 A practical approach aimed at men who wish to improve their relationship and bedroom skills.

Where Did I Leave My Keys: B08NHQ82ZM How to Keep Your Brain Sharp as You Age.

Taming The Hidden Shrew: B0BFBKPYWS How to Balance Hormones to Feel Slim, Calm and In Control.